MrsMurman

# PICTUREPEDIA

## NOTE TO PARENTS

This book is part of PICTUREPEDIA, a completely
new kind of information series for children.
Its unique combination of pictures and words
encourages children to use their eyes to discover and
explore the world, while introducing them to a wealth
of basic knowledge. Clear, straightforward text
explains each picture thoroughly and provides
additional information about the topic.

"Looking it up" becomes an easy task with
PICTUREPEDIA, an ideal first reference for all types of
schoolwork. Because PICTUREPEDIA is also entertaining,
children will enjoy reading its words and looking
at its pictures over and over again. You can encourage
and stimulate further inquiry by helping your child
pose simple questions for the whole family to
"look up" and answer together.

# INSECTS AND SPIDERS

# DK

## A DK PUBLISHING BOOK

**Consultant** Paul Hillyard
**Project Editor** Rosemary McCormick
**Art Editor** Richard Clemson
**Designer** Marianne Markham
**U.S. Editor** B. Alison Weir
**Series Editor** Sarah Phillips
**Series Art Editor** Paul Wilkinson
**Picture Researcher** Lorna Ainger
**Production Manager** Ian Paton
**Production Assistant** Harriet Maxwell
**Editorial Director** Jonathan Reed
**Design Director** Ed Day

First American edition, 1993
6 8 10 9 7 5

Published in the United States by
DK Publishing, Inc., 95 Madison Avenue
New York, New York 10016

**Library of Congress Cataloging-in-Publication Data**

Hillyard, P. D.
    Insects and spiders / [Paul Hillyard]. — 1st American ed.
    p. cm. — (Picturepedia)
    Includes index.
    Summary: Presents, in text and illustrations, the characteristics
and habits of a variety of insects and spiders.
    ISBN 1-56458-385-6
    1. Insects—Juvenile literature. 2. Spiders—Juvenile literature.
[1. Insects. 2. Spiders] I. Title. II. Series.
QL467.2.H54   1993
595.7—dc20
                                      93-19074
                                      CIP
                                      AC

Reproduced by Colourscan, Singapore
Printed and bound in Italy by Graphicom

# INSECTS AND SPIDERS

DK PUBLISHING, INC.

# CONTENTS

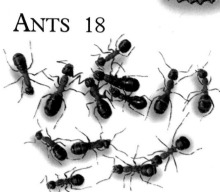

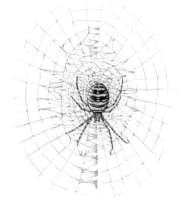

# WHAT IS AN INSECT?

*Head*

*Thorax*

*Abdomen*

Scientists think that there are more than a million known types of insect in the world and that there are many more waiting to be discovered. Most insects are rarely seen. They live hidden away from view, creeping through undergrowth, building homes in gardens and forests. But some occasionally come to live in our homes.

## Insect Features
Not all creepy crawlies are insects. Insects are identified partly by the way their body is divided into three parts: a head, a thorax, and an abdomen.

## True Bugs
Even though we sometimes call insects bugs, many of them are not. But there are creatures that are true bugs. Bugs can be identified by their mouthparts, which are formed into movable beaks used to pierce and suck food. Bugs' forewings are always hard at the base and soft at the tip.

*All insects have simple eyes that are sensitive to light.*

*Adult insects use their antennae for feeling and "smelling."*

*This insect also has two large compound eyes. Insects with compound eyes can see images and spot even the smallest movement.*

## Eat Up
Insects' mouthparts are specially designed according to their diet.

Beetles bite and chew their food. They also have jaws to grasp prey.

Flies spit on their food to dissolve it. Then they suck it up.

A butterfly has a proboscis, which is used to suck up nectar.

Mosquitoes pierce skin and suck blood.

A honeybee eats with a wide-tipped proboscis, called a "honey spoon."

## Staying Power

There were insects on Earth long before the dinosaurs arrived. The first insects came from the steamy swamps of long ago. Many were human-sized monsters, but through the ages, they got smaller and smaller.

350 to 280 million years ago

280 to 65 million years ago

65 million years ago to present day

## Ordering Insects
Scientists have divided insects into large groups, or orders. Similar-looking insects are in the same order.

Butterfly

Beetle

*This is a jeweled frog beetle, which lives in the tropical rain forest.*

*Most adult insects have wings.*

*An insect carries its skeleton outside its body in the form of a hard case, called an exoskeleton.*

*All adult insects have six legs. The legs are attached to the thorax.*

Dragonfly

Wasp

### Close Relatives
These crusty creatures are members of the arthropod family. About 900,000 arthropods are insects, but other arthropods include sea crabs, crayfish, and horseshoe crabs. Even though they are not insects, they have some insectlike features. Horseshoe crabs have compound eyes and simple eyes. Crayfish and crabs have pincers for grasping.

Horseshoe crab

Crab

Crayfish

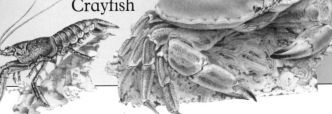

Grasshopper

# FLIES

You have probably seen a housefly zooming around your kitchen. Most people think of flies as pests – annoying little creatures that buzz around us, bite us, walk on our food, and spread disease. But in other ways, flies are a necessary and useful part of our world. They help to pollinate plants and are eaten by a variety of other animals.

A hover fly taking off

**Sensitive Flies**
Flies have surprisingly strong senses. This means they have very good eyesight and keen senses of taste and smell.

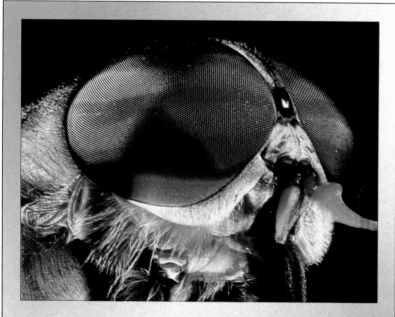

*Flies have two large compound eyes, which see colors and shapes.*

*Many flies, like the housefly, have small antennae.*

*When the fly finds liquid food, it simply sucks it up. If it finds solid food, the fly first dissolves it with special juices.*

*At the end of a fly's mouth are two pads that look like lips.*

**Nice to See You!**
A human eye has just one rounded lens. A housefly has thousands of six-sided lenses, and each lens sees a part, or piece, of a bigger picture. When a housefly looks at you, it sees you as different pieces.

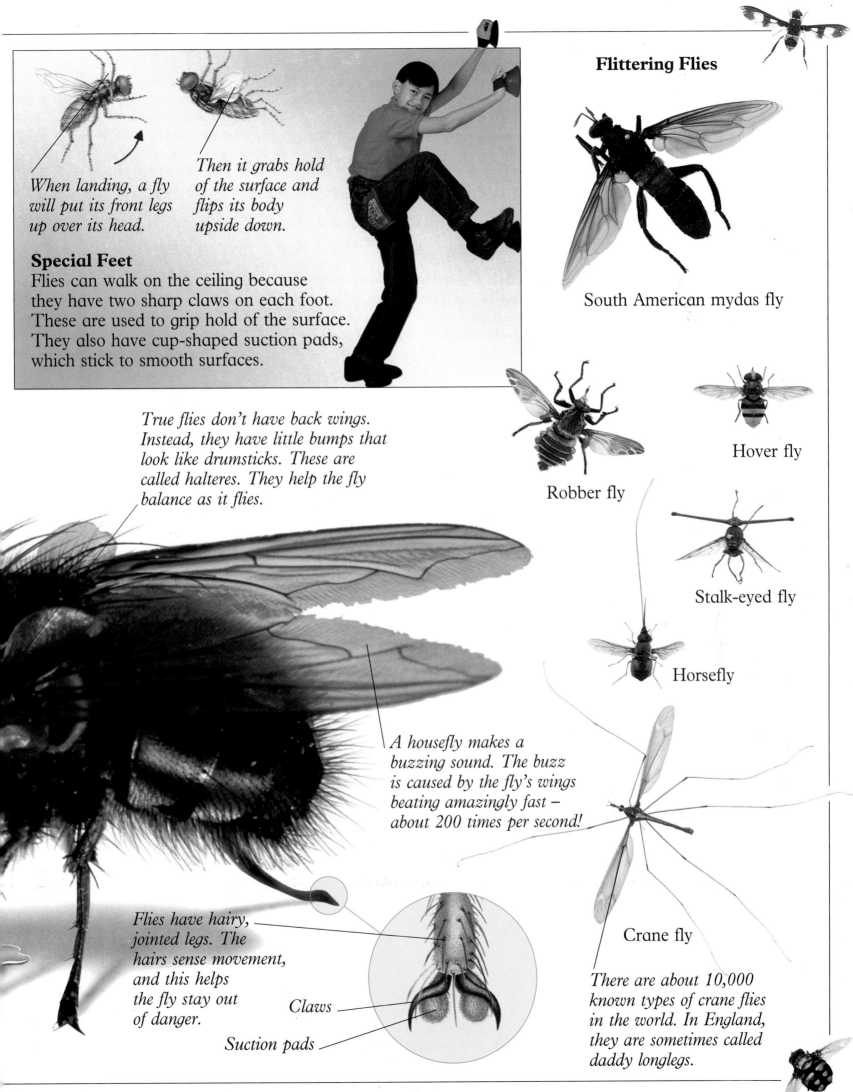

When landing, a fly will put its front legs up over its head.

Then it grabs hold of the surface and flips its body upside down.

**Special Feet**
Flies can walk on the ceiling because they have two sharp claws on each foot. These are used to grip hold of the surface. They also have cup-shaped suction pads, which stick to smooth surfaces.

*True flies don't have back wings. Instead, they have little bumps that look like drumsticks. These are called halteres. They help the fly balance as it flies.*

*A housefly makes a buzzing sound. The buzz is caused by the fly's wings beating amazingly fast – about 200 times per second!*

*Flies have hairy, jointed legs. The hairs sense movement, and this helps the fly stay out of danger.*

Claws

Suction pads

**Flittering Flies**

South American mydas fly

Robber fly

Hover fly

Stalk-eyed fly

Horsefly

Crane fly

*There are about 10,000 known types of crane flies in the world. In England, they are sometimes called daddy longlegs.*

# BEETLES

There are more species of beetles in the world than any other kind of animal. It is thought there are at least 300,000. Most are plant-eaters, but some battling beetles attack and eat other insects and are quite ferocious. Beetles can be pests because they eat valuable crops. But mostly they are helpful to us because they eat dead plants and animals and return them to the soil as important nutrients.

**Ready for Battle**
A beetle's hard outer casing acts like protective armor.

*Forewing*

**Take That!**
These fighting beetles are stag beetles. They get their name because male stag beetles have large "horns." These are really large jaws that are used for fighting like the antlers of a real stag. Males fight to defend their territory.

*The tough, black wing case protects the delicate hind wings.*

*Hind wing*

**Special Friend**
Ladybugs are beetles, too. Not all beetles can fly, but ladybugs can. They use their hind wings to fly.

*The beetle's claws help it grip.*

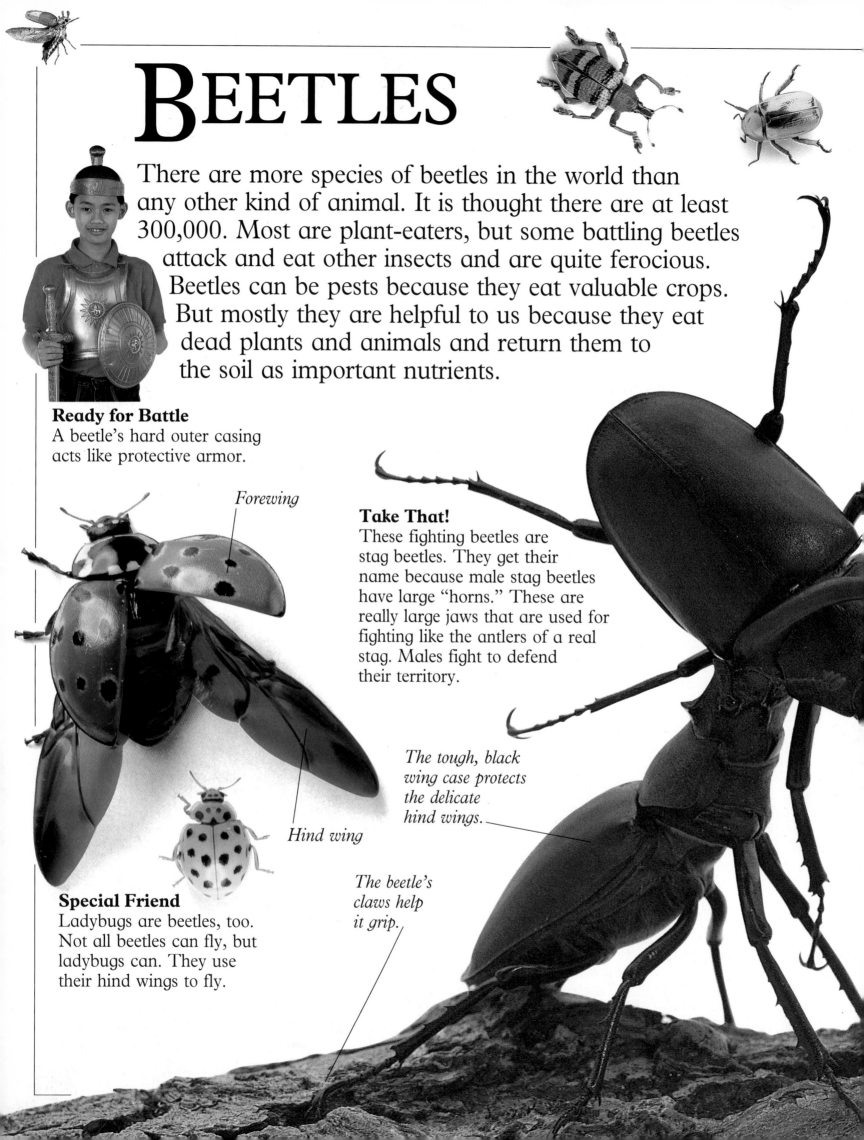

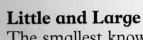

## Little and Large

The smallest known insect in the world is the feather-winged beetle. It is so small, it can sit on a pinhead. The Hercules beetle is thought to be the longest beetle in the world. It can grow up to 6.5 inches (17 centimeters) long!

## Valiant Beetles

Rove beetle

Tortoise beetle

Giraffe beetle

*Fighting males lift each other off the ground. They do this by grasping their opponent around the middle.*

## Night-Lights

Fireflies are not really flies. They are beetles. At night, the females put on a light show as they flash their tails to attract a mate. They are able to do this because they have a special chemical in their bodies.

*If it's attacked, it fires off a mixture of burning chemicals.*

Bombardier beetle

— *Hard, antlerlike jaws*

*Beetles have palps to help them sense food.*

Beetle storing dung

## Roll Over

Dung beetles go to a lot of trouble to find a safe and nutritious home for their young. They collect animal dung and roll it into large balls. They roll the dung balls all the way to their underground homes. There they lay their eggs in the dung. When the beetle larvae hatch, they discover a tasty meal in front of them!

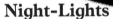

# CATERPILLARS

Caterpillars are like tiny eating machines. They spend most of their time chomping on leaves. Caterpillars are actually the young of butterflies and moths. They hatch from the eggs the adult female has laid on plants. With constant eating, they get bigger and bigger, until they are ready to change into butterflies and moths.

**A New Skin**
Caterpillar skin cannot stretch. So as it gets larger, the caterpillar breaks out of its skin. Underneath is a new, larger skin, which will last until the caterpillar needs to molt again.

*Caterpillars produce silk from special glands and force it out through a spinneret under the head.*

*The front three pairs of legs are called thoracic legs and are used for walking and clasping.*

*A caterpillar has 12 tiny, simple eyes, called ocelli, on its head.*

**Hatching Out**
The butterfly's eggs are laid on the underside of a leaf.

The egg gets darker as the caterpillar prepares to hatch.

The caterpillar bites its way out and then pulls itself free of the eggshell.

*The caterpillar's head is armed with a pair of stout jaws, called mandibles.*

*Caterpillars test food and guide it to their mouth with mouthparts, called maxillary palps.*

*The body is divided into 13 segments.*

The first meal is the eggshell, which is full of nourishment itself.

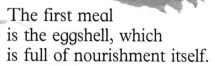

## Wonderful Caterpillars

Caterpillars can be hairy or spiny and have unusual shapes.

Tiger moth caterpillar

Cabbage white caterpillar

Emperor moth caterpillar

Puss moth caterpillar

*Like most insects, caterpillars breathe through openings called spiracles.*

*The five pairs of stumpy, suckerlike legs are called prolegs. The caterpillar uses them for clinging onto plant stalks.*

## Silkworms

Silk is produced by most moth caterpillars. But the finest silk is produced by the large white moth caterpillar, often known as a silkworm. After the caterpillars have spun themselves into a silken cocoon, they are put into boiling water. The silk is removed and spun into threads to create material for clothes.

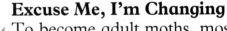

## Masters of Disguise

To avoid being eaten, some caterpillars have developed crafty disguises. The hawk-moth caterpillar looks like a deadly snake, the lobster moth looks like a raised lobster's claw, and the common sailer looks like a shriveled leaf.

Hawkmoth

Lobster moth

Common sailer

## Excuse Me, I'm Changing

To become adult moths, most moth caterpillars spin themselves a cocoon using silk, which comes out of the spinneret. Inside, they undergo astonishing physical changes.

13

# BUTTERFLIES

Butterflies are perhaps the most beautiful of all insects. It is amazing to think that a fat, leaf-eating caterpillar can become a brightly colored, fluttering creature of the air. The change happens in the butterfly chrysalis. The caterpillar's body is broken down and completely changed. After about four weeks, a fully formed butterfly emerges.

**Time to Wake Up**
The butterfly comes out of the chrysalis in three stages. During this time, it is very open to attack by hungry birds or spiders.

*1. No longer a caterpillar, a beautiful butterfly comes out of the chrysalis with its wings crumpled up.*

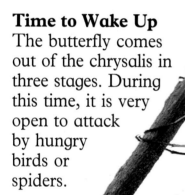

**Monarchs on the Move**
Most butterflies hatch, live, and die in one place. But when winter comes to the eastern and western coasts of North America, thousands of monarch butterflies head south to the warmth of California and Mexico. When warm weather returns to their first home, they fly north again.

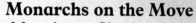

## Happy Landings

A clouded yellow butterfly comes in to land on a thistle. Butterfly flight is more controlled than it looks. The insect is able to change course instantly and make sudden landings.

*Butterflies feed through a tube, called a proboscis. This is coiled up when not in use.*

*Butterflies have clubbed antennae.*

## In the Background

Butterflies make a tasty meal for birds. But if they are able to blend in with their background, they may avoid being eaten. The open wings of the Indian leaf butterfly have a striking orange pattern. But when its wings are closed, it looks just like an old, dry leaf.

*Wings open*

*Wings closed, resting on leaf*

## Brilliant Butterflies

*2. The butterfly must stay still for some hours as blood is pumped into the wing veins to stretch the wings. Later, it holds its wings apart to let them harden.*

*3. When its wings have hardened, the butterfly is ready to fly off to find its first meal of nectar.*

Male bird-wing butterfly

Glass swallowtail butterfly

88 butterfly

## Scaly Wings

The wings of both butterflies and moths are made up of tiny scales, which overlap like the tiles on a roof. Bright colors can be used either to attract a mate or to warn predators that the butterfly or moth is not good to eat.

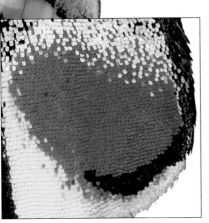

Cramer's blue morpho butterfly

# MOTHS

Most moths are night fliers, and their strong senses of smell and hearing make them well suited to a nighttime existence. They can easily find their way through darkness, and although attracted to light, they are dazed by it. Moths rest by day, and many are colored to look like tree bark or leaves so that they cannot be spotted by natural enemies, such as birds and lizards.

*Moths' antennae are straight or fernlike. They are used for smelling out nectar, or other moths at night.*

*The South American ghost moth has the biggest wingspan of any moth. Wing tip to wing tip, it can measure up to 12 inches (30 cm).*

**Wings at Rest**

One way to tell a moth from a butterfly is to see how the insect folds its wings. Butterflies close their wings upright. But most moths rest with their wings folded over their backs.

Nymphalid butterfly

White ermine moth

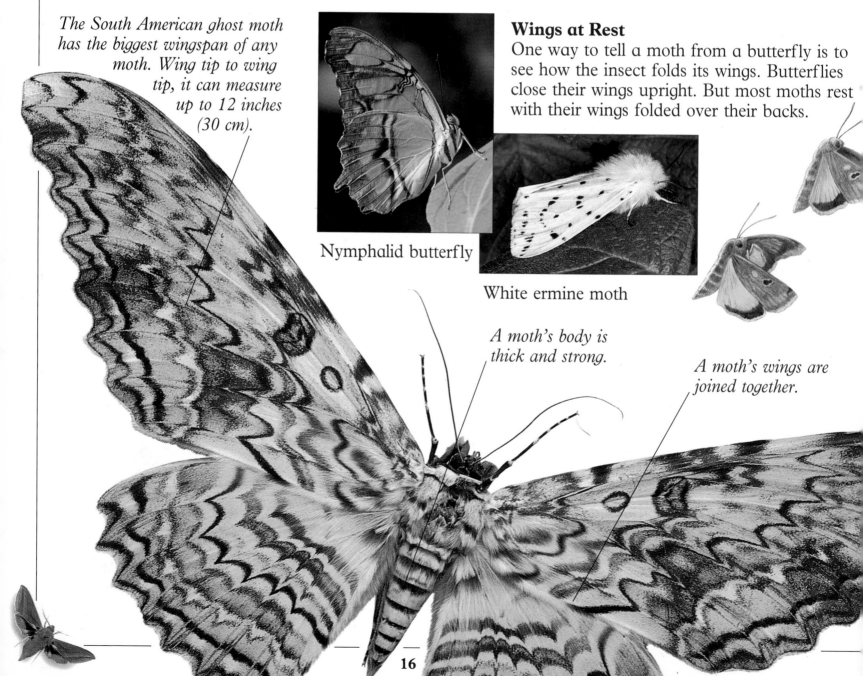

*A moth's body is thick and strong.*

*A moth's wings are joined together.*

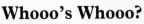
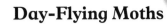

## Whooo's Whooo?

To scare off enemies, such as birds, the wing patterns of some moths mimic the appearance of fierce animals. The great peacock moth has big eyespots on its wings, which look like an owl's eyes. With these staring back at them, birds think twice before attacking!

Colombian blue-wing moth

Madagascan red-tailed moth

Verdant hawkmoth

Sloan's uraniid moth

## A Real Eyeful!

Pyraustine moths have strange feeding habits. With their long proboscises, they drink the tears of animals such as cows and buffaloes. They are so gentle that the animal's eye does not become irritated.

*The veins of the moth's wing help warm or cool the insect.*

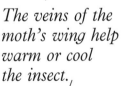

## Spot the Moth!

This geometrid moth from the jungles of Borneo looks like lichen on a tree trunk. The secret of its camouflage is not just color, but also ragged outlines and broken patterns.

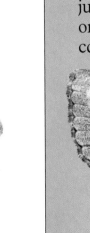

# ANTS

Ants live together in nests that are like underground towns. There may be up to half a million ants in one nest. Most of these are female and are called workers. Some workers build and repair the nest, while some are "soldiers" and guard the entrance. Others gather food for the larvae and the huge queen. Her life is spent laying millions of eggs, and the survival of the nest depends upon her well-being.

**Weaving Away**
Weaver ants make their nests in trees. They sew leaves together using a sticky silk thread produced by their larvae. The queen lives inside the leaf envelope.

*Some ants will spray a nasty chemical from their rear end if they sense danger!*

*Ants have powerful jaws, or mandibles, for chopping food. The mouth is just below the mandibles.*

*When ants meet, they "tap" antennae. The antennae contain chemical "messages" that can be passed on by touching.*

*Ants can run very fast because they have long legs.*

**Farming Fungus**
Leaf-cutting ants are the farmers of the ant world. They cut up bits of leaves and take them back to the nest. Fungus grows on the rotting leaves – and then the ants feed on the fungus!

## Left, Right!

Driver ants from South America are very fierce insects. They are nomadic, which means they are always on the move. They march in columns through the forest, killing and eating everything in their path. Here they are raiding a wasp's nest.

## Bustling Ants

Red ant

Black ant

Harvester ant

Wood ant

Dinoponera – the largest ant

## Living Larders

Some honey-ant workers spend their whole lives feeding on nectar. Their abdomens swell. Then, when food is hard to find, other workers use them as a food supply.

## Inside an Ants' Nest

The success of an ants' nest relies on the hardworking and organized inhabitants.

*Wingless workers take care of the ant larvae.*

*A network of tunnels joins the chambers in the ants' nest.*

*The queen lays her eggs in the royal chamber.*

*Seed-crushing ant*

*Soldier ant guarding the entrance*

# TERMITES

Within the insect world, termites are the master builders. Their nests are marvels of construction, specially shaped to suit the environment in which they live, whether it is the desert or the rain forest. Up to 7 million termites may live together in one nest, which can be a towering mound of mud and soil 25 feet (7.5 meters) high.

**Time for Lunch**
This anteater has food on its mind. Anteaters don't just eat ants – they eat termites, too. They use their strong claws to open nests and mounds. Their long snouts make it easy for them to reach the insects that live inside.

Inside the nest, fungus grows on the termites' dung. Termites feed on the fungus. These areas are called fungus gardens.

Food for the inhabitants of the nest is stored in special food galleries.

Deep inside each nest lives a royal couple. Their job is to keep the numbers of the nest as large as possible. The queen lays all the eggs, and the king fertilizes them.

Beneath each tower there is a cave that houses dozens of chambers. The cave can be up to 10 feet (3 meters) wide.

## Special Jobs

The nests are well organized, and each termite has a special job to do. Not all termites look the same – it all depends on what their jobs are. For example, the workers, who feed and clean the king and queen, are always blind and wingless. The soldiers, who defend them, have strong biting jaws.

Egg-laying female

Worker

## Meet the Queen

This may look like a giant sausage but it is really a queen termite. The queen is the largest termite in the nest. Her body is bloated and full of eggs. She will lay up to 30,000 eggs a day – that's about one egg every three seconds.

Young nymph

Soldier

*The walls of the nest become hard and baked by the Sun.*

Long-winged nymph

Short-winged nymph

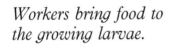
*Workers bring food to the growing larvae.*

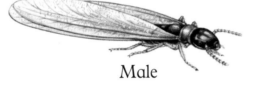
Male

Young female

## Home Sweet Home

Termites build their nests to fit in with their surroundings. In northern Australia, magnetic termites build high, wedge-shaped mounds that run north to south. This means that the scorching midday Sun shines on the knife-edged part, and the nest does not overheat.

Magnetic nest

Tree nest

*Below the main cave are cavities sometimes up to 33 feet (10 meters) deep. The termites' water supply comes from these cavities.*

## Living in the Jungle

Termites often plaster their nests high above the ground on trees. In these same jungles, other termites build umbrella-shaped nests. The sloping roof protects the nest from heavy rainfall.

Umbrella nest

# GRASSHOPPERS

Grasshoppers are known for the "ticking" sounds they make and for their ability to leap high into the air. There are more than 20,000 different kinds of grasshoppers in the world. Grasshoppers are plant-eaters, feeding on leaves and stems. Normally, they prefer to be alone. But under special conditions, they undergo a series of physical changes. They increase in size, become more brightly colored, and gather in millions to become a swarm of hungry locusts.

*The long back legs are good for leaping. A grasshopper can jump more than three feet (one meter).*

*Its legs and feet have spikes, which it uses to defend itself against enemies.*

*Grasshoppers have very keen eyesight and hearing.*

*Grasshoppers' colors help them blend in with their background.*

**Name That Tune**
Grasshoppers are good fiddle players. They make music the same way a violin produces sound. The grasshopper's leg is its bow, and the tough wing vein is the string. Crickets are also known for their musical ability. They use their wings to make sound. One wing has a thick vein with bumps on it. This is called the file. The cricket rubs the file over a rough ridge on the other wing to make cricket music.

Cricket

Grasshopper

**Chirping Cousins**
Crickets belong to the same insect group as grasshoppers. But crickets have longer antennae and like eating other insects.

## Growing Up

Female locusts lay their eggs in the sand. The babies, called nymphs, hatch and dig their way out. When they appear, they are tiny versions of their parents. In order to become fully grown adults, the nymphs molt between three and five times. After each molt, the nymphs are bigger than before. When they molt for the final time, they emerge with full-sized wings.

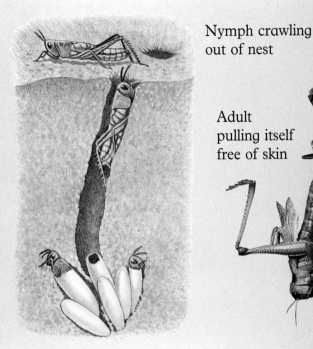

Nymph crawling out of nest

Adult pulling itself free of skin

Adult resting while its wings harden

## The Trouble with Locusts

When heavy rains fall in hot, dry regions, lush plant life begins to grow. With lots of food, large numbers of grasshoppers get together to mate. After mating, they eat all the plant life around them and grow much larger. In search of more food, they take to the air in huge swarms, devouring fields of valuable crops.

Locust-infested areas

## Extended Family

All of these insects are related to grasshoppers, but they have quite different features – and very clever disguises.

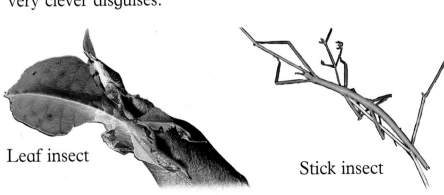

Leaf insect

Stick insect

Praying mantis

# BEES

Bumblebee

You have probably heard the buzz of a honeybee as it flies from flower to flower. During the spring and summer months, bees spend their time collecting food. There are thousands of different types of bees, and many of them live alone. But social bees, such as honeybees, live in large nests or hives. They gather nectar to be stored in the hive and turned into honey.

**Nest Making**
Some bees make their hives out of chewed leaves, mud, and animal hairs.

**Working Hives**
Hives built by people are specially made to house thousands of bees. Farmers place these hives in their orchards so the bees will pollinate the trees.

*As the honeybee moves from flower to flower, it collects a yellow powder from each one, called pollen. The bee carries the pollen back to the hive, where it is turned into food.*

*This honeybee is feeding on nectar, a sweet liquid found in flowers. It sucks out the nectar with its long, tubelike mouthparts.*

*Bees help pollinate flowers by carrying pollen from flower to flower.*

*The bee's sting is in its tail.*

## Honeycomb
Inside the hive, the bees store honey in a comb, which is made up of thousands of little six-sided cells. The bees feed on the honey during the cold winter months.

*A large hive can hold up to 50,000 bees.*

*Worker honeybees look after the young and turn nectar into the sweet liquid we call honey.*

**Buzzy Bees**

African killer bee

Orchid bee

Parasitic bee

Asian carpenter bee

## Shall We Dance?
Worker bees scout for food. When they find a good supply, they do a dance – in a figure-eight pattern – to tell the other bees where the food is. The bees in the hive then know where the food is by the angle of the figure eight and the position of the sun in the sky.

## Queen Bee
Every hive needs a queen. The queen bee mates with the male, called a drone. She then lays all the eggs. New hives are formed in summer when a young queen leads lots of workers out of the old hive to a new one.

## Royal Jelly
Royal jelly is actually bee milk. It is filled with good things like sugar, protein, and vitamins. The developing young, or larvae, of the worker bee do not get to eat the royal food – they are fed on pollen and honey. Only the larvae that are destined to become queens eat royal jelly. Because it is so rich in vitamins and proteins, people now use it to make face creams, soap, and vitamin tablets.

Royal-jelly products

# WASPS

We know that a honeybee makes honey, but what does its relative, the wasp, do? Like bees, wasps help pollinate plant life. Many wasps spend their lives eating the grubs and caterpillars of insects that are harmful to important food crops. Some wasps like company and live together in nests with thousands of other wasps. But many wasps live alone. They are called solitary wasps.

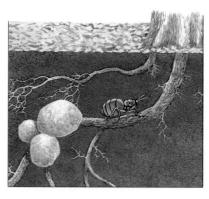

**Home in a Root**
Gall wasps lay eggs in oak roots. A swelling, called a gall, grows around the developing larva and provides it with food and protection.

American wasp

*Wasps have sense hairs on their heads, which give information about their surroundings.*

*Wasps use their antennae to measure the size and shape of each new cell in the nest as it is built.*

*The front and back wings on each side are joined together by a tiny row of "hooks." The hooks allow each pair of wings to flap as one.*

*Wasps have powerful jaws. They use them for digging, cutting, and making their nests.*

*The common wasp is between .6 to .8 inches (15 to 20 millimeters) long.*

*A wasp has a narrow waist, which separates the thorax and abdomen.*

**The Busy Potter**
The female potter wasp is really quite artistic. To house and protect her egg, she builds a delicate little pot made of mud. Then she finds food for the egg and places it inside the pot. After laying her egg, she seals the nest.

*The female puts a caterpillar in the pot.*

*When the larva hatches, it has a safe home and lots of food!*

## Paper Homes

The common wasp's nest is made from chewed wood fibers mixed with saliva to make a material much like paper. To begin with, the queen works on her own, building several layers around the egg cells in the center. Then she lays eggs in each cell. When the eggs hatch, the newly born workers help the queen finish the nest.

*The queen wasp is beginning the nest.*

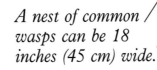

*A nest of common wasps can be 18 inches (45 cm) wide.*

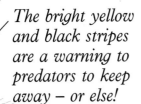

*The bright yellow and black stripes are a warning to predators to keep away – or else!*

*A wasp's sting is in its tail.*

Parasitic wasp

Giant wood wasp

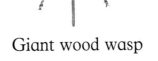

Paper wasp

## Watch Out for That Sting

Only the queen and worker wasps have a sting. They use their stings as a defense against predators and to paralyze prey.

## Tarantula for Dinner

The tarantula hawk wasp is the world's largest wasp. The female catches tarantulas and stuns them with her sting. She puts the tarantula in a burrow and lays her eggs on it. When the young hatch, they have a tasty meal.

# WATER INSECTS

Walking beside a pond on a calm summer evening, you might not notice many signs of life. But if you were to look more closely, you would find a world swarming with insects. Many insects live close to watery areas – such as ponds, rivers, and lakes – and many more live just on the surface. But there are also thousands of insects that live under the water. In fact, many insects pass from one stage of their development to another in the water.

*Water measurer*

*The water boatman uses its hind legs like oars.*

*The water boatman swims along upside down in the water and pops up to the surface to breathe.*

*Its front legs are strong and made for grasping.*

*The bug's hairy legs help it swim.*

*Whirligig beetles can fly, swim on the surface, and dive underwater.*

*This great diving beetle is a fierce hunter of small fish and insects. It can stay in the water a long time by storing air under its wings.*

*Midge larva*

*This damselfly nymph is almost ready to leave the water to spend the rest of its life in the air.*

*The fringes on the beetle's legs help push it through the water.*

*Mayfly nymphs eat plants and breathe through feathery gills on the abdomen.*

*Caddis-fly larvae make protective shells out of silk, twigs, and little stones.*

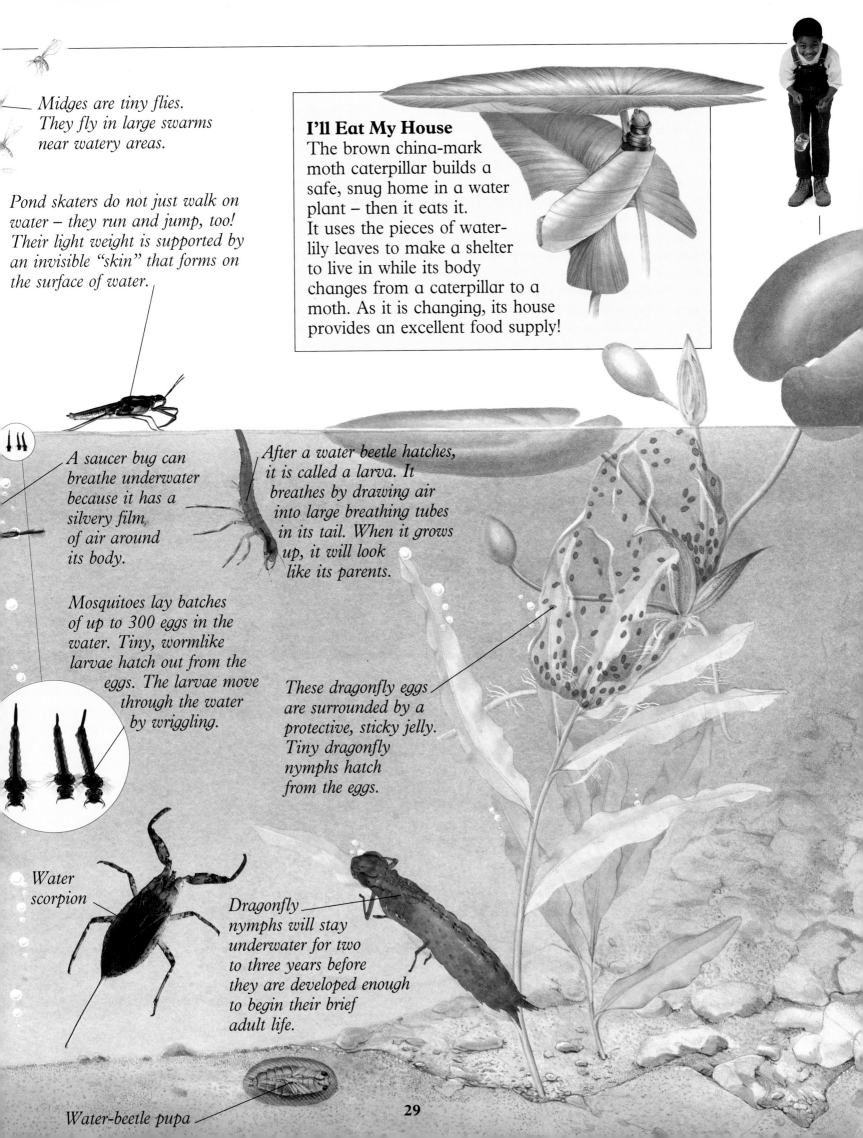

Midges are tiny flies. They fly in large swarms near watery areas.

Pond skaters do not just walk on water – they run and jump, too! Their light weight is supported by an invisible "skin" that forms on the surface of water.

**I'll Eat My House**

The brown china-mark moth caterpillar builds a safe, snug home in a water plant – then it eats it. It uses the pieces of water-lily leaves to make a shelter to live in while its body changes from a caterpillar to a moth. As it is changing, its house provides an excellent food supply!

A saucer bug can breathe underwater because it has a silvery film of air around its body.

After a water beetle hatches, it is called a larva. It breathes by drawing air into large breathing tubes in its tail. When it grows up, it will look like its parents.

Mosquitoes lay batches of up to 300 eggs in the water. Tiny, wormlike larvae hatch out from the eggs. The larvae move through the water by wriggling.

These dragonfly eggs are surrounded by a protective, sticky jelly. Tiny dragonfly nymphs hatch from the eggs.

Water scorpion

Dragonfly nymphs will stay underwater for two to three years before they are developed enough to begin their brief adult life.

Water-beetle pupa

29

# DRAGONFLIES

Many insects are good fliers, but dragonflies are truly the champions of flight. Millions of years ago, human-sized dragonflies patrolled the skies. Even today's finger-length dragonflies are quite large compared to other insects. Once dragonflies have emerged from their water-based nymph stage, they take to the air, flying at speeds of up to 35 miles (56 kilometers) per hour.

**Wing Power**
Dragonflies have strong muscles that control the base of the wings. In flight, the wings look like a rapidly changing X shape.

**Dancing Dragonflies**
To attract a mate, swarms of male dragonflies perform dances in the air.

Mating dragonflies

**Baby Dragonflies**
When the female is ready to lay her eggs, she dips her abdomen into the water. The eggs sink below the surface.

*Each pair of clear, veined wings can beat separately. This means that dragonflies can hover.*

*Dragonflies have excellent eyesight. They have two huge compound eyes. Each eye can have up to 30,000 lenses.*

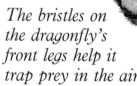

*The bristles on the dragonfly's front legs help it trap prey in the air.*

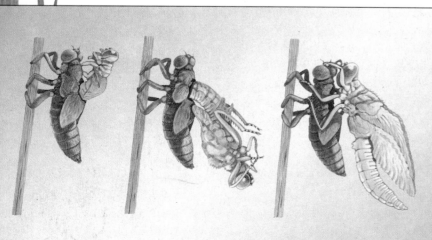

**Growing Up**
Once the fully developed dragonfly nymph has climbed up out of the water, it begins its last and most spectacular change. The nymph's skin cracks open, and an adult dragonfly pulls itself free.

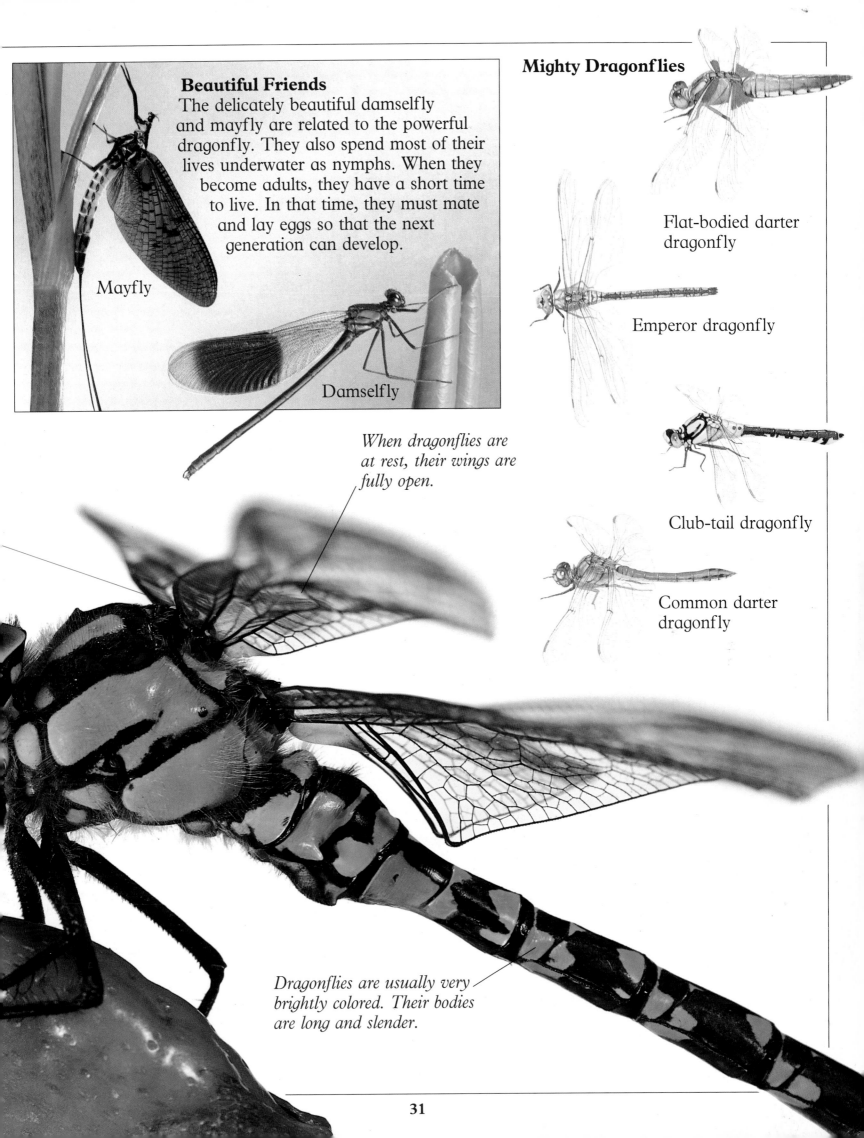

**Beautiful Friends**

The delicately beautiful damselfly and mayfly are related to the powerful dragonfly. They also spend most of their lives underwater as nymphs. When they become adults, they have a short time to live. In that time, they must mate and lay eggs so that the next generation can develop.

Mayfly

Damselfly

Flat-bodied darter dragonfly

Emperor dragonfly

Club-tail dragonfly

Common darter dragonfly

*When dragonflies are at rest, their wings are fully open.*

*Dragonflies are usually very brightly colored. Their bodies are long and slender.*

# COCKROACHES

Cockroaches can survive almost anywhere, feeding on almost anything. That is why they are one of the oldest types of winged insects in the world. They have existed on Earth about 100 times longer than people. They are often called the "rats and mice" of the insect world because they like our warm, sheltered homes and feed on the garbage we throw away.

**A Crawler with Wings**
Did you know that cockroaches can actually fly? Here you can see the cockroach's wing case.

**Warning Colors**
This South American cockroach is mimicking the color pattern of a poisonous beetle. Birds will therefore avoid eating it.

*Cockroaches are very sensitive to vibrations – they can sense a movement of less than .00000004 inches (1 millionth of a millimeter).*

*The female produces a hard egg purse, called an ootheca, to carry her eggs in. Inside the purse are two rows of eggs.*

*Wing case*

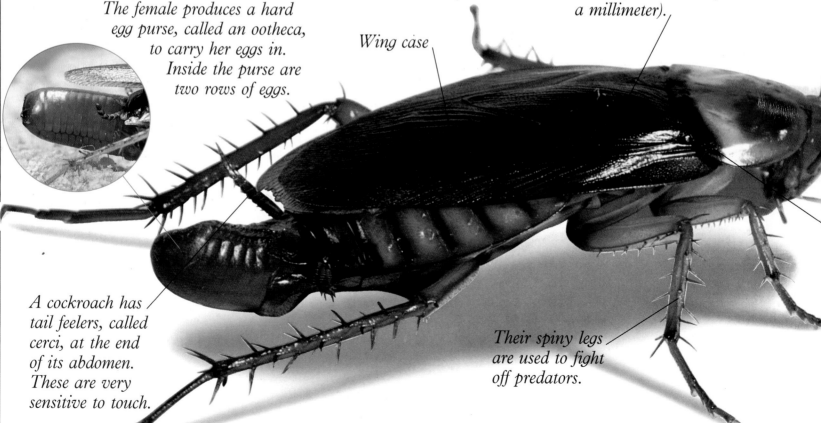

*A cockroach has tail feelers, called cerci, at the end of its abdomen. These are very sensitive to touch.*

*Their spiny legs are used to fight off predators.*

## Hidden Away

Most cockroaches never bother anyone at all. They live in all sorts of environments, such as tropical forests, caves, deserts, and under the ground.

Rain-forest cockroach

Madagascan hissing cockroach

Desert cockroach

American cockroach

Oriental cockroach

## Greedy Insects

Cockroaches are scavengers. Many of them live on plant life, but others are happy to eat the kinds of food we like to eat! Some will even eat manufactured things, such as paper.

Cockroaches eating paper packaging

Cockroaches eating cake

*Their long, threadlike antennae help them feel their way in the dark.*

*A cockroach has a flattened body, which makes hiding in narrow cracks easy.*

## Safety in Numbers

These cockroach nymphs are sticking together. The larger the group, the more protection there is for the individual nymph. Also, the bright colors on their bodies trick birds and lizards into thinking that they are either poisonous or horrible tasting!

# WEB SPIDERS

Spiders are different from insects in many ways. First, they have a different name – they are called arachnids. Unlike an insect's, a spider's head and thorax are fused together. It has four pairs of legs and no antennae. All spiders are meat-eaters. Some spiders, such as this funnel-web spider, make webs to catch their prey.

**I'll Eat You Later**
If a web spider catches a tasty insect, but is not hungry, it poisons it, but does not kill it. Then it wraps it in silk and keeps it for later.

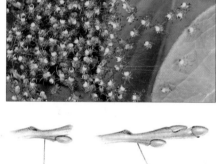

**Up, Up, and Away**
When baby spiders – called spiderlings – want to travel long distances, they take to the air. They do not have wings, but they are still able to fly. They produce a piece of silk and use it like a balloon.

*Spiders do not have bones. The head and thorax are covered by a hardened shield.*

*The spiderling suspends itself from a long line.*

*It makes a loop, which is slowly drawn up by the breeze.*

*When it's ready to take off, it cuts itself free.*

*Silk is produced through the spinnerets on the end of the spider's abdomen. Spiders use their legs to pull the silk out.*

*The saclike abdomen contains the heart, lungs, silk glands, and reproductive parts.*

**Garden Surprise**
Scientists think that insects are attracted to spiders' webs because the webs reflect ultraviolet light. Insects use ultraviolet light to find their way and to find food.

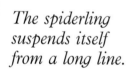

## Ready to Attack

This Australian funnel-web spider is one of the world's deadliest. Here it is poised, ready to attack! When spiders catch their prey, usually insects, they use their "fangs" to poison and kill them. The funnel-web spider, like most spiders, uses its strong digestive juices to dissolve the insect's insides so the spider can suck it dry.

## Spiders and Webs

The net-casting spider lives in trees, mostly in jungle areas. To catch prey, it spins a sticky net and throws it over passing insects.

*Most web spiders have eight simple eyes, called ocelli. But even so, they cannot see very well.*

## Making a Web

Making a web takes time and special care. Spiders only spin new webs when the old ones become untidy or damaged.

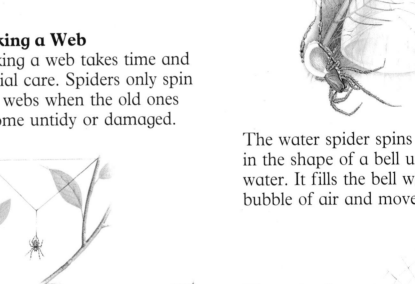

The water spider spins a web in the shape of a bell under the water. It fills the bell with a bubble of air and moves in.

*A spider has a pair of graspers, called palps, on each side of its mouthparts. They are used to seize prey.*

The web of the orb-web spider looks like a target. It takes about an hour to spin a complete web.

*Spiders have eight legs.*

*Even though spiders do not have ears, they can "listen" to the world around them through their webs. The webs are very sensitive to vibrations in the air.*

The female purse-web spider lives in a silken pouch. When an unsuspecting insect lands on top, the spider bites through the pouch and grabs it.

# HUNTING SPIDERS

Not all spiders spin a web and wait for their prey to get caught in it. Many catch their prey without the use of silk. They are called hunting spiders. Some patrol their territory, looking for insects to pounce on. Others crouch in burrows and wait for prey to wander past. Unlike web spiders, hunting spiders have strong legs for jumping and keen eyesight so that they can easily spot their victims.

*Chilean red-leg spiders are among the largest hunting spiders in the world. They can grow to 5 inches (13 cm) long. They hunt at night and feed on mice and small birds.*

*A hunting spider has eight simple eyes on the front of its head. It hardly has to move its head to be able to see in all directions.*

## Hide and Seek

A tree-trunk trapdoor spider is a tricky creature. After it has made a safe, secure burrow with its powerful jaws, it constructs a trapdoor at the entrance. Unseen, it lies in wait behind the trapdoor, ready to leap upon any unsuspecting insects that might crawl by.

*The hairs on the spider's body are very sensitive to vibrations made by moving prey.*

*It has strong legs for digging burrows.*

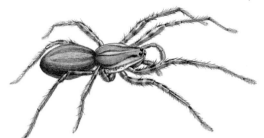

## Happy Hunters

### Long Jumpers

Hunting spiders need good eyesight because they have to see and chase after their next meal. Many hunting spiders can measure exactly the leap they must make onto their victim as they run along after it.

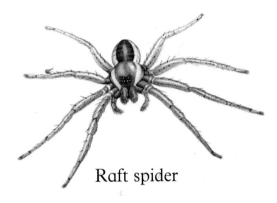

Brazilian wandering spider

Crab spider

### Full Speed Ahead

Wolf spiders hunt during the day. This Australian wolf spider lurks at the entrance of its silk-lined tunnel ready to race full speed after prey.

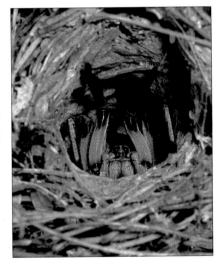

Raft spider

Wood-louse spider

### Take Aim, Fire!

A spitting spider spits when it is hungry. When it spots an insect, it spits a stream of sticky gum from each fang. This glues the insect to the ground until the spider can arrive to eat it.

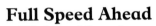

# SCORPIONS

Scorpions are known to be deadly. But their reputation is worse than their sting. Like spiders, scorpions are arachnids. They live mostly in hot countries – in deserts or rain forests. They are shy creatures, spending their days in burrows where it is cool. They have even been known to creep into people's shoes to get away from sunlight.

**I'm Not Afraid of You**
Meerkats think scorpions are rather tasty. When they catch a scorpion, they bite off its stinging tail and devour the meaty part of the scorpion's body.

*The tail is jointed so that it can bend.*

*The poison is stored in two glands in the swollen part of the sting.*

*The sting tip is very sharp for piercing the skin of prey.*

*Scorpions have four pairs of simple eyes, but they rely more on smell than on sight.*

*This is a South African creeping scorpion. Its color helps it blend in with its background.*

*The front legs of scorpions are armed with pincers. These are used to grab and hold prey.*

# Stinging Scorpions

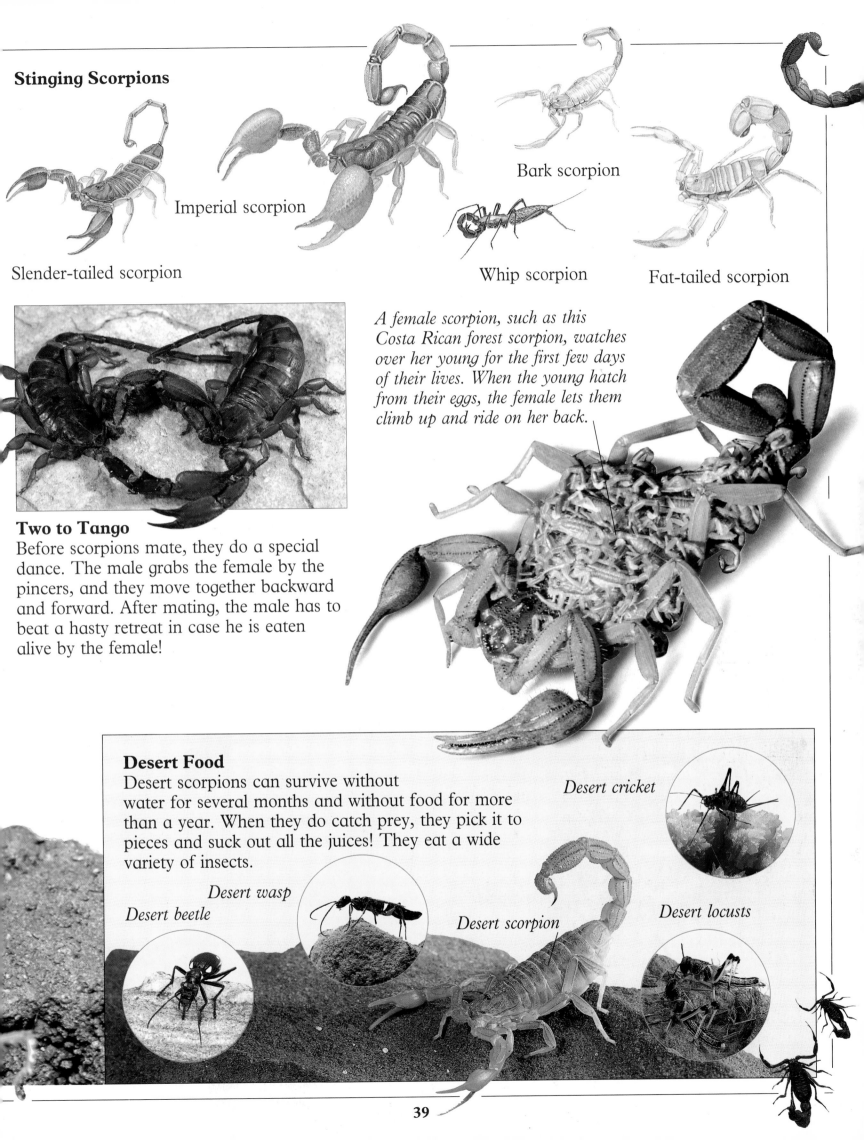

Imperial scorpion

Bark scorpion

Slender-tailed scorpion

Whip scorpion

Fat-tailed scorpion

*A female scorpion, such as this Costa Rican forest scorpion, watches over her young for the first few days of their lives. When the young hatch from their eggs, the female lets them climb up and ride on her back.*

## Two to Tango
Before scorpions mate, they do a special dance. The male grabs the female by the pincers, and they move together backward and forward. After mating, the male has to beat a hasty retreat in case he is eaten alive by the female!

## Desert Food
Desert scorpions can survive without water for several months and without food for more than a year. When they do catch prey, they pick it to pieces and suck out all the juices! They eat a wide variety of insects.

Desert cricket

Desert wasp

Desert beetle

Desert scorpion

Desert locusts

# CENTIPEDES AND MILLIPEDES

**Walk This Way**
"Millipede" means "thousand feet," but no millipede has more than 400 feet. Millipedes move with a slow, wavelike motion using up to 22 pairs of legs.

Centipedes and millipedes have an external skeleton as insects do, but in other ways are very different. Their bodies do not divide into a separate head and thorax, and they do not have wings. Above all, they are many-legged creatures and can have anywhere from 9 to 200 pairs of legs. You would think that, with so many legs, they might occasionally trip over themselves. But they have amazing control over every single leg.

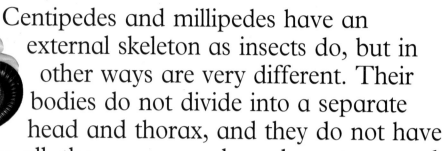

*A millipede's body is divided into segments. Each segment has two pairs of legs.*

*The hard outer skin is called a cuticle.*

**Curled Up**
The giant African millipede coils itself up into a tight ball when it feels threatened. By curling up, it protects the soft underside of its body.

*A millipede has a row of stink glands along the side of its body.*

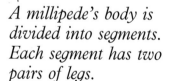

Pill millipede

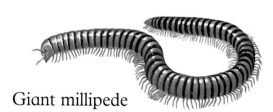

Giant millipede

**Forward, March**
The name "centipede" means "one hundred feet." Centipedes move along very rapidly with fewer than half their legs touching the ground at any one time.

**Plant-Eaters**
Millipedes only eat plants. They burrow through the soil, using their strong jaws to scrape and chew rotting leaves.

**Meat-Eaters**
Centipedes are fierce hunters. They eat grubs, insects, and worms. They have even been known to eat lizards, mice, and toads.

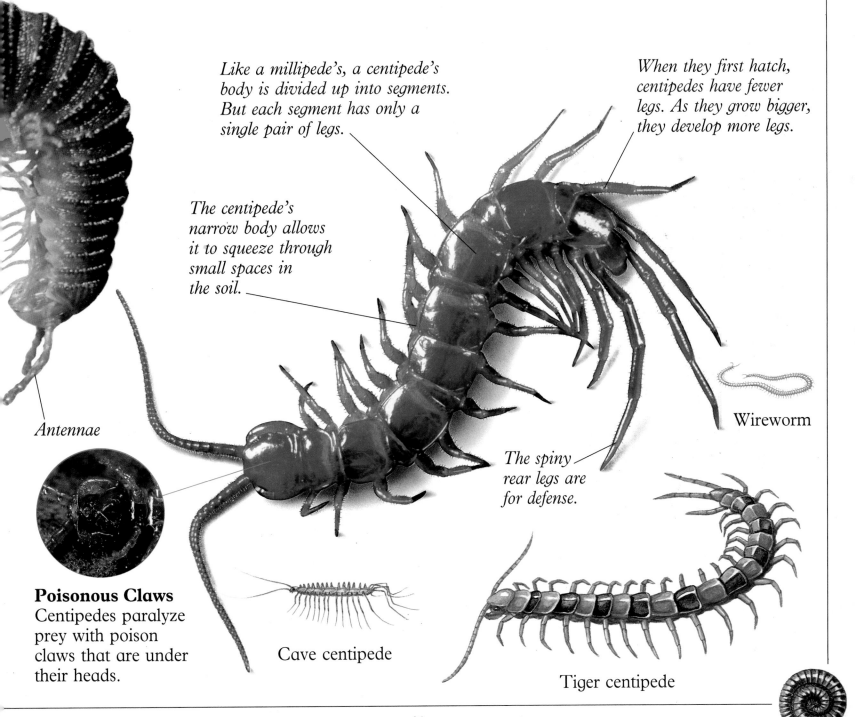

*Like a millipede's, a centipede's body is divided up into segments. But each segment has only a single pair of legs.*

*When they first hatch, centipedes have fewer legs. As they grow bigger, they develop more legs.*

*The centipede's narrow body allows it to squeeze through small spaces in the soil.*

*Antennae*

*The spiny rear legs are for defense.*

Wireworm

**Poisonous Claws**
Centipedes paralyze prey with poison claws that are under their heads.

Cave centipede

Tiger centipede

# INSECTS IN THE HOME

Even though you may not see them, there are probably insects in your home. They like the warmth, shelter, and food a house can provide. Most are not harmful to us, just annoying. But some are so dirty, they may cause illnesses. Others can eat away at the structure of our homes, weakening roofs, floors, and stairs.

## Silverfish
Silverfish are often found in kitchens. They are actually quite useful in that they eat up any small bits of food we drop in our homes.

## Evil Weevil
The grain weevil is actually a beetle. In many parts of the world, it is a serious pest because it eats its way through large amounts of stored grain.

## Flour Beetles
These beetles are quite often found in people's kitchens eating their way through bags of flour.

## Barklice
Barklice usually live under bark on trees. They live on the small molds that grow there. But they have been known to eat books, too!

## Woodworms
Woodworms are not actually worms – they are the larvae of beetles. The beetles lay their eggs mostly on wooden furniture. When the eggs hatch, the larvae burrow into the wood and feed on it.

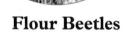

## Flea Larvae

The tiny white flea larvae live on bits of old food found on rugs and carpets.

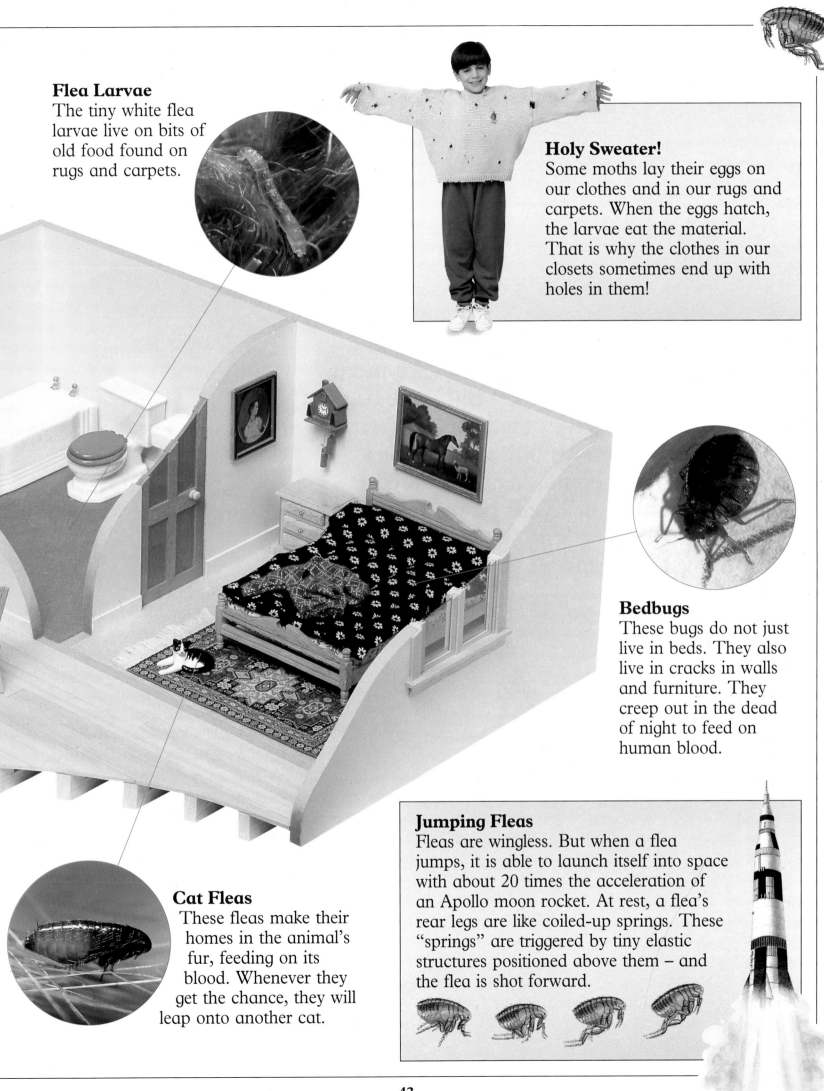

## Holy Sweater!

Some moths lay their eggs on our clothes and in our rugs and carpets. When the eggs hatch, the larvae eat the material. That is why the clothes in our closets sometimes end up with holes in them!

## Bedbugs

These bugs do not just live in beds. They also live in cracks in walls and furniture. They creep out in the dead of night to feed on human blood.

## Cat Fleas

These fleas make their homes in the animal's fur, feeding on its blood. Whenever they get the chance, they will leap onto another cat.

## Jumping Fleas

Fleas are wingless. But when a flea jumps, it is able to launch itself into space with about 20 times the acceleration of an Apollo moon rocket. At rest, a flea's rear legs are like coiled-up springs. These "springs" are triggered by tiny elastic structures positioned above them – and the flea is shot forward.

# INSECTS THAT SPREAD DISEASE

Throughout history, diseases spread by insects have caused the deaths of millions of people. Today, in many parts of the world, the bite of an insect is no longer such a serious problem. We now have medicines that can cure many previously incurable illnesses. But there are still some places, such as the tropics, where insects can be a serious threat to people's health. When you go out hiking in wooded areas, it is best to tuck your pants into your boots and wear long sleeves to avoid being bitten by insects.

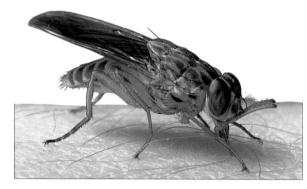

**Sleeping Sickness**
The African tsetse fly drinks human and animal blood, spreading a disease, called sleeping sickness. First this causes extreme tiredness. Then it affects the body's nervous system.

**Poison Kiss**
The South American triatoma bug (sometimes called the kissing bug) causes a skin complaint called Chagas' disease. The infected person develops large, dark patches on the skin.

**The Body Louse**
Lice are bloodsuckers. There are three kinds of lice that live on humans, but the most common is the body louse. It lives on people's clothes and spreads a disease, called typhus. Typhus causes severe aches and pains.

**Keep Out!**
Nets are draped over beds in the tropics so that people can sleep without being bitten by mosquitoes. This simple measure has saved many lives.

44

## The Black Death

Several hundred years ago, rat fleas spread a disease through Europe known as the Black Death. Hundreds of thousands of people died.

## Disease Spreaders

Sheep tick

Blackfly

Rabbit flea

Soft tick

## Lyme Disease

Deer ticks can carry Lyme disease to human beings. (Ticks are not actually insects, they are relatives of spiders.) Lyme disease causes soreness and swelling of the joints.

## Malaria

Mosquitoes are probably the best known of all biting insects. But only one type, the anopheline, carries the disease malaria. Malaria is spread when the female anopheline sucks blood from the human body, and tiny organisms enter the bloodstream. The first signs of malaria are chills and high fevers.

*The mosquito has only a single pair of wings, like other kinds of flies. Its wings beat so fast that they make a high-pitched, whining sound.*

*Mosquitoes have compound eyes.*

*Featherlike antennae*

*The mosquito's proboscis is entering human skin and sucking up blood.*

*The female anopheline mosquito always sticks one pair of legs up in the air when she is feeding.*

*The female mosquito's abdomen fills with blood as she feeds. The female must have a blood meal before she can lay her eggs.*

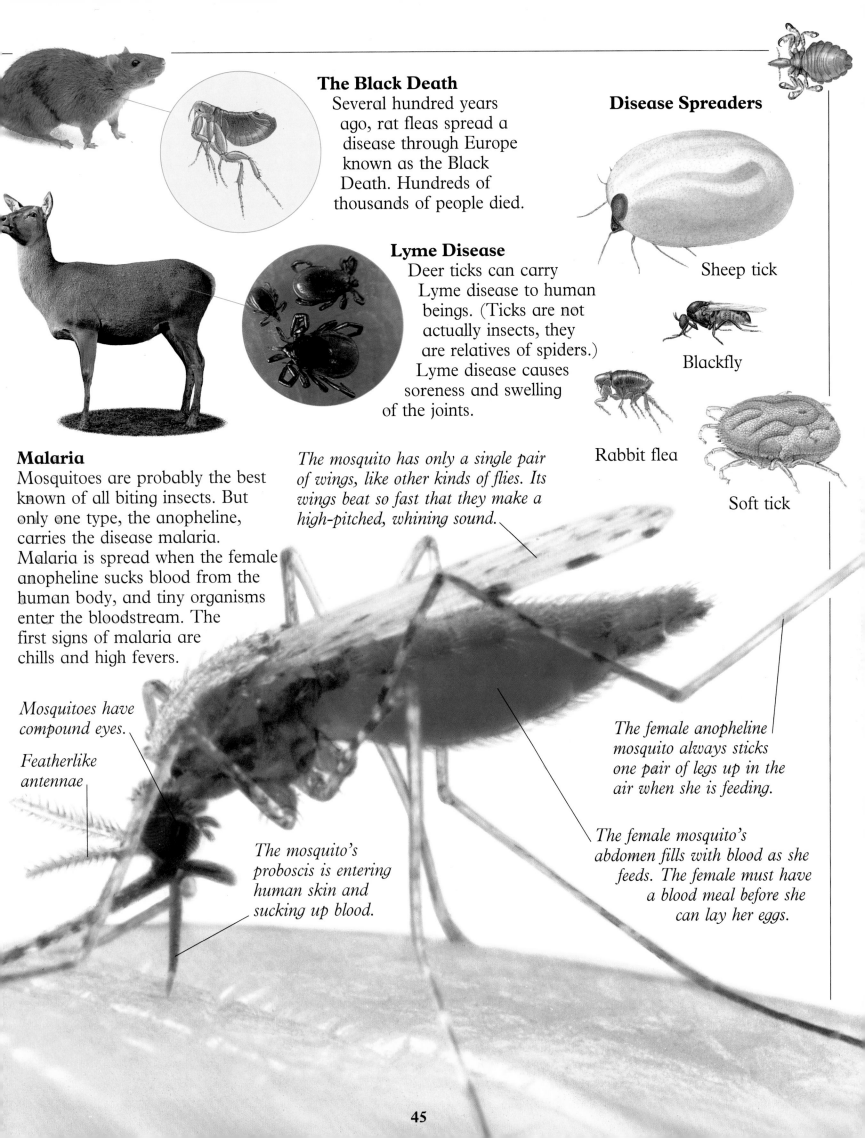

# INSECTS AND PEOPLE

We do not usually think about the number of insects crawling around our world. That is probably just as well, because scientists think that for every person, there are about 200 million insects! Insect numbers have been affected by both natural and human-made pest controls. But there is no doubt that they have proved themselves to be formidable survivors.

### Moving Overseas
Insects have been accidentally carried all over the world in cargo ships and planes.

### Insect Presents
Without these creeping creatures, our planet would not have its wonderful variety of fruits and beautiful flowers.

### Cactus Killers
Insects are used to control unwanted plants. In Australia, the prickly pear cactus took over vast areas of farmland. So farmers let loose cactus moth caterpillars. They ate the prickly pear, clearing the land.

### Insects in the Food Chain
Insects are an important part of the animal food chain.

The beetle…is eaten by a lizard…which is eaten by a bird…which is eaten by a wildcat.

## Pollution Problem

Insects are being found with wings or bodies that are not properly formed. This is because they have had contact with chemicals that have found their way into the rain and then rivers and lakes.

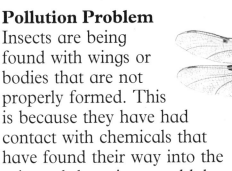

## Save Our Homes

Like mammals, insects are affected by the destruction of forests and jungles. If their home is threatened, so are they.

## Bug Busters

Insects feed on other insects, naturally controlling their numbers. Because many chemical pesticides harm the environment, insects are sometimes used to control other insects. This is called biological control.

## Bee Cure

Some insects can provide cures for certain illnesses. Bee venom is used to treat illnesses that affect the joints and blood circulation, such as rheumatism and arthritis.

# GLOSSARY

**Abdomen** The last of the three sections that make up an insect's body.

**Antennae** The feelers on an insect's head.

**Arachnids** Spiders, ticks, and scorpions.

**Arthropods** A group of animals that have external skeletons.

**Biological control** A way of keeping down pests by letting other animals loose to feed on them.

**Bugs** Insects with beaklike, piercing mouthparts and wings that are thick at the base and thin at the tip.

**Cerci** Feelers on an insect's abdomen.

**Chrysalis** The protective covering of certain insects. A caterpillar turns into a butterfly inside a chrysalis.

**Compound eye** An insect eye made of thousands of tiny lenses.

**Cuticle** The hard outer skin of an insect.

**Environment** The surroundings in which an animal lives.

**Exoskeleton** The skeleton or shell on the outside of an insect's body.

**Fertilization** The union of male and female cells in order to produce young.

**Generation** Animals that are born at the same time.

**Gland** An organ that produces chemicals.

**Head** The first section of an insect's three-part body.

**Halteres** The parts of a fly that help it balance in flight.

**Hive** A house or box for bees to live in.

**Larvae** The young of insects.

**Mandibles** Insect jaws.

**Mimic** To copy the look or behavior of another animal.

**Molting** The process of shedding old skin.

**Nectar** Sugary fluid produced by flowers to attract insects.

**Nutrient** Any substance needed for growth and health.

**Nymph** Stage of growth in some insects, such as grasshoppers, that comes before adulthood.

**Ocelli** Simple eyes that have single light-sensitive lenses. Caterpillars have 12 ocelli.

**Ootheca** The egg case of cockroaches and some other insects.

**Palps** A pair of mouthparts that are used for holding on to food.

**Pesticide** Chemicals used by humans to kill insects.

**Pollinate** To carry pollen from one flower to another and so fertilize it.

**Predator** An animal that kills and eats other animals.

**Proboscis** A tube-shaped mouthpart used for sucking.

**Pupa** The growth stage that many insect young must go through in order to become adults.

**Reproduction** The process by which living things produce offspring.

**Scavenger** An animal that feeds on rotting matter.

**Segments** The separate sections of an insect's body.

**Spinneret** Silk-producing organ in spiders and caterpillars.

**Swarm** A huge gathering of insects, such as bees or locusts.

**Thorax** The middle section of an insect's three-part body.

**Ultraviolet light** Light that is invisible to the human eye.

**Venom** Poison that insects and spiders inject into prey or enemies by biting or stinging.

**Vitamins** Substances in food that help living things to grow and stay healthy.

## Acknowledgments

**Photography:** Andy Crawford and Dave Rudkin.

**Additional photography:** Tim Ridley, Jerry Young, Dave King, Frank Greenaway, Kim Taylor, Colin Keates, Jane Burton, and Neil Fletcher.

**Illustrations:** Sandra Doyle, Roy Flooks, Mick Gillah, Norman Lacey, Michael Woods, Richard Manning, Maurice Pledger, and Sean Milne.

**Models:** Donks Models.

**Thanks to:** Caroline Brooke, London School of Hygiene and Tropical Medicine, Scallywags, and Norrie Car Child Model Agencies.

# INDEX